EX LIBRIS

A. EBBEN

PANORAMIC
SOUTH AFRICA

PANORAMIC
SOUTH AFRICA

cna

CENTRAL NEWS AGENCY LTD
CNA Building, Laub Street, New Centre,
Johannesburg, 2001

Reg. No.: 01/02033/06

First edition 1980
Second impression 1983
Third impression 1984
Fourth impression 1985
Fifth impression 1986
Sixth impression 1987
Seventh impression 1988

Designed by Walther Votteler, Cape Town
Photosetting by McManus Bros. (Pty) Ltd, Cape Town
Reproduction by Unifoto (Pty) Ltd, Cape Town
Printed and bound by Leefung-Asco Printers Ltd, Hong Kong

ISBN 0-86977-117-5

INTRODUCTION

With Cape Agulhas as her southernmost point and the Limpopo River marking her northern extreme, South Africa has a surface area of 1 140 519 square kilometres. Her dimensions are such that she could encompass West Germany, France, the Netherlands and Belgium. Britain is but a fifth of her size.

West to east, from Port Nolloth to Durban, across the southern African subcontinent, measures 1 300 kilometres reaching from the chilly South Atlantic in the west to the warm currents of the Indian Ocean in the east.

In view of the tremendous impact of western technology and culture on the landmass between these two seas, it is amazing to realise that it was but 400 years ago that white men first anchored off its shore. But even before Jan van Riebeeck and his three small ships made landfall in Table Bay, southern Africa had a history of human occupation that went back thousands of years.

For perhaps as long as 10 000 years or more the Bushman alone held this land to be his domain and he gathered and hunted freely from the bounty of the veld. Some existed for part of the year as 'Strandlopers' (beachcombers) gathering from the sea to satisfy their needs. And so they lived, changing nothing of the world about them but the rockfaces upon which they expertly daubed natural pigments, a testimony to their presence in the land.

Then, some 4 000 years ago, the Hottentots (Khoi) came south with their herds of cattle and sheep. Although pastoralists, their numbers were not so great and the natural resources of the land were such that real conflict between Hottentot and Bushman was not an issue.

Later still came the black man, urging his cattle southwards in search of grazing. He was part of a population explosion in central Africa and he needed water and pasture and land to till. His arrival on the African subcontinent brought him into direct conflict with the long-established Bushmen and Hottentots. His cattle competed with the antelope for the sweet grasses and scattered waterholes of the veld and the Bushman naturally turned his poison arrows to these usurping herds which stood docile in the face of the diminutive hunter.

In time the Bushman was to succumb all but entirely to the latecomers, both black and white. A handful survive in the country's least hospitable northern areas where the

Kalahari sands penetrate. The Hottentot, on the other hand, was to be assimilated both racially and culturally by the more purposeful people who needed land for their crops, their cattle and for their growing populations.

And so it can be seen that even then as events unfolded, one could look to the land to find the motivating forces, the factors that would drive men to war, to seek their fortunes on the *ververlate vlaktes* (wide open spaces), to create cities built on gold and diamonds, to seek a home – in South Africa.

Van Riebeeck founded a settlement at the Cape on instruction from Amsterdam and the long hand of overseas control was to find in time its colonists slowly wriggling from its grasp. The men who wanted to escape the presence of the Dutch East India Company were men of the earth. They turned inland in search of freedom, but even more they sought a place where they could cultivate the soil and see their cattle grow sleek.

But beyond the confines of Table Mountain, the Cape is not cattle country. The *fynbos* type of vegetation is soon replaced by *suurveld* (literally sour land) and for this very reason the black Bantu-speaking peoples had not settled south of the Kei River. They had instead broadened their influence on the Transvaal Highveld and in Natal where their grain flourished and the sweet *imfi* cane grew tall. The Zulu chief, Shaka, had already scythed the neighbouring peoples, binding about him a nation of warriors with broad-bladed assegais. The Xhosa to the south of them were also a proud people with a special regard for their cattle; so were the Venda, the Tsonga, the Pedi, the Sotho and Tswana who lived here too.

As the trekboers from the Cape pushed north, they did not find what they needed until they reached the Kei: sweet grass and sweet water. But the land they coveted was already peopled. And the conflict that arose was in essence that of herder against herder for the limited available resources. The bloody wars and centuries of conflict that followed are well chronicled and in them are already discernible the faint yet distinct impressions of what was to come.

Then, in 1859, a five-carat diamond was found on Erasmus Jacob's farm 'De Kalk'. Almost overnight the South African panorama was transformed from a rural outback into an increasingly urbanised and highly-complex industrial entity. Diamonds injected, along with new blood from overseas, the heady influence of the profit motive – they also placed new pressures on the land. The miners had to be fed.

The diamonds of Kimberley may have provided the impetus for urbanisation and change, but it was gold that was to sustain it. In 1886 gold was found on what came to be known as the Witwatersrand. South Africa's destiny was ascertained: she was committed to industry, mining and commerce. And, simultaneously, she was forced to seek solutions to the problems already visible in her earlier history: the need for land and the need for its optimum use.

When Britain, tempted by the new-found resources and apparent wealth of southern Africa, tried to change her desultory presence to outright control, a new breed of men, the Afrikaners, rallied to repulse her. It took time and there was no outright success, but eventually they prevailed. An identity born of the soil, nurtured by the fight to assert itself, now had a place to assert itself in.

By the turn of the century, South Africa was not only seeking its independence but also dispensations that would assure the future. There are over 24 million people in South Africa today. Tomorrow there will be many more. South Africans, black and white together, must solve the problems that have been evident from the start. Less than 12% of South Africa is arable. Most of it is semi-desert. It is vital that the land and her available resources be used in such a way that the country can feed the people who will tend the machines and interpret the ticker-tapes, who will convert the immense store of mineral wealth into a more fulfilling life for everyone who lives here.

South Africa's record so far is remarkable. She exports her surplus maize to the rest of Africa; in good years she is self-sufficient in wheat. From the inhospitable Karoo, sheep provide wool and mutton for a greedy world market. Despite the fact that she lacks water, she has ambitious schemes that will change dry savannah into verdant farmland. Her fruit graces the tables of the world

Within her boundaries lies 58% of the world's gold, 19% of the world's gem diamonds; immense deposits of coal, of iron, of base metals. Nature has blessed her with immeasurable mineral resources but it is to the land that she must look to ensure the future. Just as land was the essential source of conflict and problems four centuries ago, so it is today.

Few cities in the world can boast such a landmark; fewer still such a beacon, which appears here rosy-coloured above a wine-dark sea.

Table Mountain was named by Portuguese navigator Antonio da Saldanha in 1503, who was probably also the first European to make a recorded ascent of the 1 000 metre massif. In his time there would have been a far greater profusion of indigenous flowers and shrubs crowding its slopes with soft colour: a number of heaths *(Ericaceae)*, the world-renowned silver tree *(Leucadendron argenteum)*, exuberant wild orchids – the 'disas' exclusive to the south-western Cape Province, and, of course, the many varieties of colourful and unusual protea *(Proteaceae)*, South Africa's national flower.

Today many well-worn routes lead to its table-top summit and for those not inclined to walk or climb, a cable-car offers an easy ascent. But the centuries have taken their toll of the mountain slopes and many of the plants that one views from the top today are recent arrivals that challenge the indigenous flora, though modern-day conservationists have succeeded in halting the tide and protecting what remains in nature reserves.

The most dramatic view of the mountain is undoubtedly that presented to travellers approaching Cape Town by sea, but a creditable second-best for viewers on land is from the beach at Bloubergstrand, seen here clustered with 'vygies' *(Mesembryanthemum)*.

Table Mountain . . . beacon to every wand'ring bark

Panoramic view of Cape Town from the Foreshore

In 1703 Simon van der Stel informed his 'Council of Seventeen' that 'the new church on the Heerengracht, except for the tower,' was completed. But the Cape Town of which Van der Stel spoke no longer exists in a form which he would recognise. The Heerengracht (Gentleman's Walk) he referred to is now Adderley Street and where it originally ran down to a small inlet called Roggebaai a new Heerengracht carries city traffic.

In 1937 the task of reclaiming land from the sea was begun, a mammoth undertaking with a view to enlarging the city's inadequate harbour and extending its commercial centre. The operation was completed in 1945 and represented one of the greatest feats of its kind. Covering 194 hectares of what is now known as the 'Foreshore', it has completely transformed the profile of the bay and only a line of palm trees standing just beyond the present railway station marks the shoreline Van der Stel knew.

Mostert's Mill, built in 1796, Mowbray

Lutheran Church, Strand Street, Cape Town

Profusion of colour – flower sellers off Adderley Street

A view up Long Market Street to the mosque, the oldest in the country

Percussionists in the Khalifa display

An exterior in the partly-restored Malay Quarter

The Muslim faith exercises an all-pervasive influence on the lives of its followers. The Malay population of South Africa, the majority of which lives in Cape Town, remains staunchly orthodox in its observance of the injunctions of the prophet Mohammed.

The Cape Malays mark the high point of their religious calendar during the fast of Ramadan – a month of purification of body and soul. For 30 days all people over the age of seven may neither eat nor drink between sunrise and sunset. It is a time of meditation and atonement. The end of Ramadan is celebrated in the feast of Eid Dul Fitr.

To outsiders, the Khalifa display is the best known of the Cape Malay rituals. Performed in public, the display's symbolic meaning is that of the power of faith over the flesh. Today, however, the traditional piercing of flesh as practised in the Khalifa is widely frowned upon and regarded as being more sensationalist than of any truly religious significance.

The now traditional fez, introduced by Turkish missionaries in 1861

Camps Bay's white beach sweeps below Lion's Head on the Peninsula's Atlantic seaboard

Clifton's four famous beaches

The 144 kilometre-long marine drive skirting the Cape Peninsula leads to scores of unspoilt beaches as it winds through residential suburbs lying on either side of this mountainous promontory.

But only hardened habitués of the western seaboard will be found swimming in the deep-chilled water which washes the beaches at Clifton and Camps Bay. The rest come to lie on the sands and absorb the sun and view.

Beyond Camps Bay stretch the 'Twelve Apostles', the chain of peaks which extends southwards towards Cape Point.

On Clifton Beach

Flanked by the Sentinel and Chapman's Peak is Hout Bay in whose tranquil waters a colourful fleet of fishing boats finds shelter. At the harbour they unload crayfish for the export market. From here, too, fishermen put out to sea in winter to catch the snoek *(Thyrsites atun)* which appear off this coast. Fresh, dried, salted or smoked, this Cape delicacy has a noble flavour – and a good measure of romantic Cape tradition associated with it as well. The quayside auctions are colourful and boisterous and conducted in a mixture of languages, dialects and special slang.

From Hout Bay village a magnificent drive carved into the sheer slopes of Chapman's Peak leads towards Cape Point.

Guarding the entrance to Hout Bay is the Sentinel . . .

14

. . . and Chapman's Peak

Cape Point, highlight of the Cape of Good Hope Nature Reserve

'The fairest cape in all the circumference of the earth' . . . 'the Cape of Storms' . . . 'the Cape of Good Hope' . . . these descriptions by early mariners record their feelings on rounding Cape Point – on reaching the end (albeit not quite the southernmost tip) of Africa.

It was a rare moment which was to elude one of its most fervent seekers and thus produce perhaps the most poignant tale in the Point's history. Twice Diego Cão had searched for the tip of Africa and in January

1486 he was a bare 700 kilometres from his goal when his fleet of tiny ships took shelter in the lee of a rocky outcrop (now known as Cape Cross in Namibia). History does not reveal why he chose this spot to plant another *padrão* – but it was to be the last of the stone crosses which mark his passage down Africa's west coast. Cão died shortly afterwards and his ship returned to Europe.

But by a wry twist of fate the cross was to reach the

Cape Point, where Africa's crooked finger embraces False Bay

Fynbos splashed with *sewejaartjies (Helichrysum vestitum)*

Cape of Good Hope after all. In 1893 Captain Becker of the German ship *Falke* spotted the cross and removed it to have it restored. But first he called at Cape Town for repairs to his ship and it was thus that the *padrão* completed its mission – 407 years after its master's death.

Bontebok, rare antelope of the western Cape

17

Protea cynaroides, the giant protea

Cape sugarbird (*Promerops cafer*)

Pincushion proteas (*Leucospermum cordifolium*)

18

Once the property of the Kirsten family, the estate was unanimously approved as the site of the National Gardens in 1913, and today occupies some 485 hectares on the slopes of Table Mountain.

This incomparably beautiful setting provides sanctuary for a great variety of the Cape's growing things – contributing to the conservation of what the pioneering Swedish botanist Carolus Linnaeus described as 'a paradise on earth . . . more valuable than the wealth of Solomon or Croesus'. Linnaeus's enthusiasm is understandable, even to a layman – of the six floral kingdoms in the world, that of the Cape is richest by far. It has been estimated that in the Cape Kingdom there are some 1 300 different species per 10 000 square kilometres.

The conservation of this natural heritage has become a matter of great concern for some 60 per cent of the original fynbos (the local name for this flora) has already been destroyed by human interference of one kind or another.

Kirstenbosch, a tribute to the wonders of the Cape Floral Kingdom

Banked by mountains, the sparkling waters of Gordon's Bay rush onto long, smooth beaches
previous page: Groot Constantia (built 1692, restored 1790s and 1920s)

The Portuguese called it *Cabo Falso*, for their navigators in the approach from the east frequently mistook it for the entry to Table Bay. Rounding Cape Hangklip, False Bay balloons into an expanse of warm water protected from the fury of winter's storms and harbouring some of the Cape's most popular beaches and holiday resorts.

A night drive along False Bay's coast will expose an almost perfect horseshoe of twinkling lights amongst which are those of Gordon's Bay in the east and St James in the west.

Evoking an age of gentlemen in striped bathing suits, the gracious hotels and colourful wooden changing booths of St James are for those who wish to experience the charm of unhurried, old-world seaside vacations. At the other extreme, Gordon's Bay is a modern resort with luxury accommodation clustering around white-beached coves.

Changing booths at St James

Towards the close of the eighteenth century the Cape wine industry was most successfully represented both here and in Europe by the fashionably sweet Muscadel grape imported from Spain and cultivated to perfection in the vineyards of the Constantia Estate, founded by Governor Simon van der Stel.

The arrival at the Cape near the end of the seventeenth century of the Huguenots greatly advanced the industry and over the 300 years or so that followed, locally produced wines have acquired an international reputation for quality. Cape brandies, sherries and port are even more esteemed and rank among the finest in the world.

But this success has not gone unmarked by disaster: in the 1880s disease all but wiped out the Cape vineyards making it necessary for the farmers to replant with insect-resistant stock. Since then the industry has gone from strength to strength, although for climatic reasons it is still limited to the relatively small winter-rainfall area of the Cape.

Men of the Boland

From wicker baskets . . .   . . . to wine cellars

Lanzerac, one of the most famous of the historic farms of the winelands

Orchards and vineyards spread over the bountiful Paarl Valley

'The Pines', Hex River Valley

'Rhone', gracious homestead in the Franschhoek Valley

26

'Waboomsrivier', Breede River Valley

The Dutch settlement at the Cape grew rapidly and by 1657 only five years after landing, Jan van Riebeeck began building for himself a 'fine double-storeyed house' at what is now Rondebosch. Less than 20 years later, Simon van der Stel had founded the village of Stellenbosch and by the turn of the century free burghers of French and Dutch origin were living as far inland as Tulbagh.

Wherever they settled they built homesteads and from these early buildings evolved the style known today as 'Cape Dutch'. It is a gracious and functional architecture characterised by elegant gables, cool thatch and gleaming whitewashed walls. The gable came from Holland but was well-adapted to conditions at the Cape where examples range from the classic to the baroque.

The use of whitewash arose initially from the mistake of the settlers trying to recreate the ethos of the Netherlands in the Cape setting. Their first houses were of naked brick and had golden-coloured tiled roofs. But, when the brickwork began to crumble beneath the cold pelting rain of the Cape winter, the need for plaster became apparent. To this end they burnt sea shells to make lime plaster. A coat of whitewash to add a waterproof finish led to the familiar, heavily plastered, gleamingly white walls.

The British fort in Kogman's Kloof near Montagu

Famous above all for its table grapes – the black-skinned Barlinka and golden Hanepoot – the Hex River Valley ('Valley of the Witch') presents a sudden and breathtaking splash of colour as the traveller descends the mountain pass that divides the parched Karoo from the Boland.

This fertile valley first featured in the records of the Dutch East India Company in 1709 when one Roelof Jantz van Hoeting was granted farming rights. By the

Franschhoek Valley from the pass

end of that century six farms occupied the better parts of the valley and today there are more than 150 farmers in this area, specialising in table-grape production. The industry centres on the town of De Doorns.

The name of the valley is said to come from a story which originated on the farm Buffelskraal. According to this legend a young girl, Eliza Meiring, set her various suitors the task of scaling the highest peak of the Matroosberg which rises 2 460 metres. In fulfilling her whim her true love, it is said, fell to his death. Deranged by guilt and shock, she too plunged down the slopes and was killed and her tormented spirit wanders still among the mountains.

The Hex River Valley known for its fine table grapes

Deserted farmhouse beneath snow-capped mountains near Touws River

The 'Lord Milner', Matjiesfontein

Beyond the Matroosberg lies the Little Karoo and the beautifully restored village of Matjiesfontein. Here in the 1880s James Douglas Logan offered good food and cheer to passengers waiting for the steam engine to cool down after the long haul out of the Hex River Valley. These were the beginnings of the 'Lord Milner' which was ultimately to accommodate visitors from around the globe – among them the Sultan of Zanzibar and Lord Randolph Churchill. The restored hotel continues the tradition established in Logan's day.

The 'Laird's Arms', Lord Milner Hotel

The Karoo holds a special attraction for the city dwellers who occasionally race across its broad plains. It is an essentially dry region – rain rarely falls, the air is crisp and temperatures fluctuate greatly. Plants have had to adapt to withstand the rigours of this climate and a unique flora has evolved. Here grow strange, thick-leaved succulents, while ephemerals leave their seeds scattered in the soil awaiting the rain that sparks off a brief but spectacular life cycle – from seed to mature plant in a matter of weeks.

Long before man evolved, the Karoo was a lushly vegetated swamp filled with strange creatures now extinct. Their remains, trapped in layer upon layer of mud and clay, were later compressed into rock. It is within these sealed archives of the Karoo System that palaeontologists today seek the rich fossil records that can help reveal the missing pages of the past.

For thousands of years the Bushman hunted in the Karoo, his poisoned arrows felling migrating herds of springbok, blesbok and wildebeest. Then came the trekboers who gradually asserted themselves, claiming the few natural watering holes for their cattle. In time the Bushman was destroyed. In recent decades sheep have helped slowly turn much of the Karoo from a fragile grassland to semi-desert. The Karoo already encompasses over a third of South Africa; it threatens to encroach upon a greater and greater area unless careful measures are taken to prevent this.

The Floriskraal Dam surrounded by the arid and undulating topography of the Karoo

Merino sheep jostle

Clouds promise . . . windmills provide

Cacti at the Sheilam Gardens near Robertson

Graaff-Reinet – after Stellenbosch and Swellendam – is the third oldest country village in South Africa. Here at the end of the eighteenth century the frontiersmen asserted their independence from the authorities at the Cape and overseas. They objected to the way in which those far from the frontier considered the tense situation should be handled and the years between 1795 and 1806 were ones of strife. Today Graaff-Reinet, known as the 'gem of the Karoo', is peaceful. It was once the scene of a prosperous ostrich feather industry. Although ostrich feathers went out of fashion with the advent of the motor car, its fertile soils and ample water make it the agricultural centre of the Karoo.

Coloured workers' houses, Graaff-Reinet

Karoo farmhouse near Fraserburg, beneath the characteristic flat-topped ridge

Shelter from the noonday sun, Graaff-Reinet   *overleaf:* Valley of Desolation near Graaff-Reinet

Nieu-Bethesda, some 50 kilometres north of Graaff-Reinet

Karoo countryside . . . between Noupoort and Colesberg

Hendrik Verwoerd Dam, Orange River

On the Cape's north-eastern frontier with the Orange Free State lies South Africa's most ambitious answer to her most pressing problem – lack of water. Here is the 'Orange River Scheme', a multi-purpose plan to take water from the mightiest dam envisaged in the project, the Hendrik Verwoerd Dam, to the arid and sere countryside many miles around.

With a planned capacity of 6 000 million cubic metres, the maximum height of the dam wall will be 73 metres above the river-bed. The wall is 914 metres long – making it the second-longest in Africa, and incorporated within the structure is a hydro-electric power station consisting of four units, each with a capacity of 80 megawatts.

Wind and watercourses have played with these mountains as man might work with clay. For more than 400 million years they have torn and scarred this sandstone massif, creating the bizarre and wonderful formations for which the Cedarberg is famous.

On rock faces the Bushmen have left paintings that are an exuberant image of their world, delighting the curious rambler. The air is aromatic with buchu (Rutaceae), pines, rooibos (*Aspalathus linearis*), and, of course, the cedars for which these mountains are named.

Three hundred years ago reports reaching Jan van Riebeeck told of the rich adornments worn by the Nama people and this suggested to the inhabitants of his early Dutch settlement that the legendary wealth of the Monomotapas might be beyond the Cedarberg. A party set out and crossed the Cedarberg but the only gold beyond the mountains was that of the golden daisies of Namaqualand, which still flower every spring.

The Cedarberg, too, has its flowers. Above the snowline of the peaks grows the rare and wonderful snow protea (*Protea cryophila*) – a plant which has resisted transplanting and refuses to survive out of its familiar hostile environment.

Then there is the *Leucospermum reflexum* – one of the pincushion family – a magnificent shrub which bears more than 100 bold crimson flowers from the upward thrusting branches.

Besides the rare and unusual, within the Cedarberg can be found many species of flowering plant unique to the southern reaches of the western Cape. For those who seek wilderness, the Cedarberg is a perpetual source of wonder.

'The Arch', one of the many famous formations in the Cedarberg

Namaqualand in flower . . .

Modern version of a traditional Hottentot hut

For a few short weeks each year Namaqualand comes alive with a profusion of colour. The territory's spring flowers which carpet the otherwise unembellished plains with abundant but short-lived glory, attract thousands of visitors.

The once-a-year show is related to many factors but perhaps the major – and most fascinating – is the dry climate which dictates the brief but flashy growing season. This dryness is in turn dictated by events many thousands of kilometres away – in the icy expanses of the Antarctic's Southern Ocean. It is here that the deep-chilled waters of the Benguela Current begin their journey across the sea depths, travelling gradually northwards until they meet with Africa's southern tip where part of this cold river of water is deflected and sweeps along the west coast. As the water wells up from the depths it cools the air and limits the amount of moisture it can carry, keeping much of southern Africa's western region thirsty.

In Namaqualand the plants are geared to this reality and their entire life-cycle is encapsulated in one short spurt of growth when the climate is at its most benign: and if sufficient rain falls it transforms the landscape into a celebration of colour.

. . . and the *gousblom* seem to stretch forever

The cheetah – fleet of foot and sleek of body

Black-backed Kite (*Elanus caerulus*)

Springbok, familiar sight in the drier parts of South Africa

44

The Kalahari Desert . . . southern Africa's sand basin

Stretching some 3 200 kilometres from the Orange River in the south to the Congo in the north and from the Etosha Basin in the west to central Rhodesia is the world's largest unbroken expanse of sand – the Kalahari sand mantle.

This vast basin of sand covers an area of over one million square kilometres yet millennia ago it was even bigger. Today the mantle is not entirely unbroken: at several places the underlying rock systems protrude through the sandy surface. Throughout the system, however, the sand varies from one metre to over 100 metres in depth.

In the north where the rainfall is somewhat higher the sand is blanketed in grass but as one moves southwards conditions become more parched and the exposed sand is brick-red.

Where South Africa borders on Namibia and Botswana, part of this Kalahari area has been set aside as the immense Gemsbok National Park which supports a surprising variety of wildlife.

Lion in the Kalahari

45

As the Orange River flows to its delta on the Atlantic coast it sweeps briefly northwards around one of South Africa's most desolate areas, the Richtersveld. Few people know this region for it is barren, inhospitable and almost impossible to penetrate.

Simon van der Stel journeyed here on his expedition to Namaqualand in 1685-86 in a vain search for treasure. According to Hottentot (Khoi) legend, however, there *is* treasure in the Richtersveld for here lives their deity, Heitsi Eibib. In the Wondergat, a yawning cave near the Orange River, he is believed to guard his riches and anyone daring to enter his cave will surely die.

Van der Stel was the first person to note the massive kokerbooms *(Aloe dichotoma)* which are such a conspicuous feature of the Richtersveld. He recorded how the Bushmen used the hollowed-out branches of this plant as quivers ('kokers') for their poisoned arrows.

Little rain comes to this northern frontier: at Goodhouse on the Orange River annual rainfall is a sparse 51 mm. It is also the hottest area in South Africa and temperatures recorded at Goodhouse show a daily average of 39° centigrade. The village's apparently ironic name arises from a corruption of the Hottentot *'Gu-daos'*, which means sheep path, and for those who eke a living in these parts sheep are their only livelihood.

But the future promises wealth for this area. The hostile landscape holds great mineral deposits of copper and tin, to name but two of her potential riches. It was copper which prompted one of South Africa's first ventures into mining when in 1852 she began to exploit the copper reserves of Namaqualand. Before very long the Richtersveld, too, will see mining development.

The *kokerboom (Aloe dichotoma)*

The Orange River in expansive mood

Goodhouse . . . badlands

The Augrabies Falls plunges some 150 metres in its granite gorge

In the silent and brooding Richtersveld tufts of grass provide sparse ground cover. Yet besides the grasses there is a host of other plants not readily detectable by the uninitiated: among them are tiny plants which are highly reduced, their small leaves mimicking the colour and texture of their environment to such an extent that they appear no more than pebbles until the occasional rainfall coaxes them briefly into flower.

This is an unforgiving habitat: those plants and creatures which do not adapt simply do not survive and everything to be found here is therefore suited in some marvellous way to the hostile climate and terrain.

South Africa as a whole is dry, but in the Richtersveld the lack of water is particularly severe, limiting where people may live and the extent of their herds. There are a handful of natural springs, notably at Lekkersing and Kuboos, and the government has sunk a number of boreholes to help alleviate the position.

The Richtersveld is an essentially Coloured area with over 2 000 people living thinly scattered over the region. However, around the permanent watering places small villages have sprung up so that where possible the children can attend school while the men take the cattle, sheep and goats far afield.

A typical dust storm swirls over the Richtersveld

Two of the most charming old villages of the Cape are Arniston and Elim.

These small villages with their simple cottages, thatched and end-gabled in old Cape tradition, have a time-worn quality. Elim, founded in 1824 as a mission station, was named after the biblical resting place of the Israelites after crossing the Red Sea. Arniston was originally called Waenhuiskrantz ('waggon-house-cliff') because of the immense sea-cave near by but its name was later changed to commemorate the *Arniston* wrecked here in 1867.

The fishing village of Arniston

Fish dries in the sun on Arniston beach

Cape gannet *(Morus capensis)*

Charming homesteads at Elim mission station   *overleaf:* Waenhuiskrantz

The Riviersonderend Valley

It has been estimated that with the optimum use of the land, South Africa can indeed feed her growing population for years to come.

South Africa's winter wheatfields roll along the coastal plains of the south-western Cape Province, at the foot of successive mountain ranges. It is an area collectively known as the 'Over-berg', or the place 'over the mountain'.

The names given to these districts fully illustrate the romance and optimism of their early settlers: 'Rivier-sonderend' means literally 'river-without-an-end' – a comforting feature in this often drought-stricken area: 'Botrivier' comes from the Hottentot name for the river 'Couga', which means abundant butter, or fat – hence 'Bot' from the Afrikaans 'botter'.

For the hardy farmers and their families who struggled over the mountains in the early days of the colony, these undulating lands meant not only soil to till and a place of their own, but escape from the control and censure of the authorities at the Cape.

Chaff attracts birds after the wheat harvest

Wheatfields at Langhoogte, near Botrivier

The once prosperous and thriving 'capital' of the Overberg was Swellendam, the third oldest town in South Africa. It was established in 1746 by the Dutch East India Company to help administer its *'Verre Afgelegene Districten'* (the remote districts), and confirmed the Company's expanding colonial enterprise.

In keeping with the rebellious mood in Europe, settlers in outflung parts of the Cape Colony also asserted their independence of established authority. Some 50 years after its creation, the citizens of Swellendam too demonstrated their concern for their livelihood by declaring a republic. The step was provoked, in a moment of heady outrage, at the decision of the Cape authorities to cancel a long-standing wheat-buying agreement. Wheat was then, and remains, the major industry of the area.

The protest was short-lived but the industry has survived to the present with such a degree of success that whereas before 1968 South Africa had to import wheat, she is now able to produce all her own requirements – both in the winter wheatlands and elsewhere.

Swellendam itself, once the last outpost of civilization, has not survived unchanged. In 1865 a disastrous fire levelled much of the town, destroying many of the fine old buildings which bore testimony to its once flourishing trade.

Sweeping wheatlands of the Caledon-Swellendam area

Humble cottage near Caledon

In 1780, Hendrik van Zyl, searching amongst the foothills of the Swartberg for cattle strayed from his herd, stumbled upon one of southern Africa's greatest natural wonders – the Cango Caves.

Water, percolating through soft limestone, formed huge caverns – and over aeons a wonderland of hanging rock was born. Light reflected from the pinnacles of stalagmites and the icicles of stalactites creates a kaleidoscopic spectacle. The caves exhibit nearly every known calcite formation: flowstone walls and curtains, rimstone pools, tiny calcite flowers and straws and even the calcite-sheathed skeletons of bats.

Almost 200 years after they were discovered, the Cango Caves yielded a new system which has been aptly named the Cango Wonder Cave. It far outshines the splendour of the more widely known system. Now the question is whether to reveal it to the public and, more importantly, how to protect it from the vandalism that stripped the original caves of their most beautiful ornamentation.

Some of the myriad formations that grace the Cango Caves

Young ostriches being herded near Middelplaas, Little Karoo

Racks of drying apricots near Ladismith

Amongst the most dramatic land formations of the Cape are the mountains of the Swartberg range and the basaltic pillars of the Valley of Desolation.

The Swartberg is a series of imposing gorges, chasms and peaks made accessible by mountain passes of which the most spectacular is the Swartberg Pass, built by Thomas Bain and opened in 1888.

Through the range the Gamka River has cut a truly remarkable gorge which can only be examined on foot. Along its course it reveals the intense geological folding which this region underwent in the past.

Where the river cuts through the mountains lies the remote valley known as 'Die Hel'. Its name is said to derive from a comment by a government stock inspector who said: 'It's a helluva place to get into and a helluva place to get out of. And I think we'll call it Hell from now on.'

Gamkaskloof, Die Hel

Spectacular geological folding revealed on the Swartberg Pass

Between the Outeniqua Mountains and the Indian Ocean lies the famed Tsitsikama Forest. Growing down to beaches rich with shells, and warm waters teeming with marine life, the forest itself is woven through with clear streams, cleft by lush, green kloofs and canopied by a dense tapestry of leaves.

There are more than 100 species of indigenous trees in the forest, several of which provide rare and beautiful hardwoods such as stinkwood. Perhaps the best known is the yellowwood whose honey-coloured timber is popular for furniture, flooring and ceilings. This relatively soft-wooded tree is the giant of the forest, its moss-bearded branches towering above the other species to a height of 50 metres and more. Some estimates place the age of certain of the yellowwoods at over 2 000 years.

Subject to none of the grazing pressures which most elephant herds in Africa today experience, a protected herd roams the Knysna forests in freedom. Rarely seen, for they are but few, these elephant are said to be amongst the largest of their kind.

The old 'Passes' road, completed by Thomas Bain in 1882, runs almost directly through the forest and offers an unrivalled experience of the Tsitsikama.

Primeval splendour of the Tsitsikama Forest

A beach in the Robberg Nature Reserve, Plettenberg Bay

The Cape Almanac of 1858 observed: 'The roads to Knysna from every point of access are of the most difficult description. The road from the west through George is intersected by dangerous rivers and heights almost precipitous. On the north it is belted in by a rugged, almost impassable range of mountains, and to the east, on the Uitenhage side, it is shut in by impenetrable forests and impassable rivers, by a country known only to a few hunters, and abounding in elephants and buffalo.'

Although the merits and demerits of the freeway through the Garden Route have been hotly disputed, the tarred highway makes Knysna and her wide lagoon, the Heads and the surrounding forests accessible in a way that was simply impossible before its construction.

The waters of the lagoon on which the town is built are, for the most part, tranquil – rendering more spectacular the crashing seas at the foot of the Heads, those two rock masses that stand at the harbour entrance.

Before the area was opened to road and rail, the harbour was a loading point for ships coming to fetch the fine timbers of the surrounding forest. Naval launches were built here during World War I, but the rise of other ship-building ports has left Knysna harbour little more than a shelter for holiday craft.

Beyond the Knysna Heads lies the fury of the open sea

Wilderness coastline

An aerial view of Knysna

Hotel at Plettenberg Bay

A Xhosa youth whose ancestors traditionally lived north of the Kei River

There are over 5,5 million Xhosa people in southern Africa and they are concentrated in Transkei, Ciskei and in the urban centres of South Africa.

Apart from the Bushmen and Hottentots, the Bantu-speaking Xhosa were the first black people to clash with white settlers as they moved northwards in their search for grazing.

Yet prior to these bitter conflicts over land, there had been more peaceable contact between black and white. In 1593 a Portuguese ship, the *Santo Alberto*, was wrecked near the Umtata River and the survivors reported the presence of Xhosa tribes in the vicinity.

In the eighteenth century, survivors of another shipwreck married with the Xhosa along the coast. Today their descendants may be found amongst the Lungu and Mhole clans. A white girl from this group of survivors actually married a Mpondo chief – in a South African turnabout of the legend of Pocahontas.

Ciskei landscape once wooded but now rolling grassland

On their arms these Xhosa women wear several metal bracelets which are believed to have medicinal properties. Pipe-smoking, as can be seen in the photograph, is not confined to men; custom decrees that a woman may smoke but only after she has borne a certain number of children. The married woman (left) wears an apron over the long skirt she wore as a maiden.

The great turbans of cloth now considered part of the 'traditional' dress of the Xhosa are a relatively recent innovation. The familiar sight of people swathed in ochred blankets is 'new' too. Prior to the introduction by the European of factory-made cloth, Xhosa women dressed in skins.

Time off from the day's labours

A Xhosa maiden, her naked breasts a sign of her unmarried status, brings thatch for repairing a roof

Xhosa youth leads a heavily laden wood-cart home

Xhosa girls await their turn at a flour mill, Butterworth

Rustic living near Elliot, northern Cape

Abakwetha – 'circumcised boys'

Despite the impact of Western culture in the lives of many South African blacks, traditional rites and customs continue to have meaning. Whereas in the cities and towns many have sought to discard the obligations imposed by tradition, in the rural areas its influence is particularly strong.

For Xhosa boys, circumcision and its attendant rites proclaim manhood. Protected by cow-hair necklaces, the initiates enter a no-man's-land between boyhood and adulthood; their spiritual limbo is symbolically reinforced through their physical seclusion in special huts remote from the village. During this period they are instructed in the ways of men – their rights and obligations.

The circumcision ceremony marks the peak of the initiation ritual. The boy must face the knife without fear or flinching. If his courage fails he brings dishonour to himself and his family.

A further period of seclusion follows giving the wounds time to heal. It is during this time that the young men, smeared with white clay, are taught the dance of the *abakwetha*, the dance of the circumcised boys.

Some 2 000 metres above sea-level, on the slopes of the Drakensberg, lies Barkly East, the tiny village which has the dubious distinction of being one of the highest and coldest settlements in the country. Here, near the border between South Africa and Lesotho, the temperature drops below freezing point for an average of 93 days every winter.

The construction of the Barkly East railway line was begun in 1902, but when partly finished its course was radically altered by distant events. The original plan was to take the line to the top of a 100 metre chasm through which runs a river, and then construct what would have been the highest bridge in South Africa.

Unfortunately the bridge materials went down with the ship carrying them to South Africa when it was sunk by a U-Boat during World War I. Pressing ahead with the building of the line all the same, the present eight reversing stations were constructed, finally reaching Barkly East.

The community is still served by this rail link which staggers upwards with a gradient of 1 in 36, an arduous trip for the steam locomotives which formerly laboured up its track.

Since 1978 the line has been dieselised, but the route still provides a panoramic view of some of the most exciting landscapes in the country.

The majority of Barkly East's residents are connected in one way or another with the village's major activity – sheep farming. On the precipitous slopes of the surrounding mountains can be found some 600 000 sheep, many of which become victims of either the sub-zero temperatures or rustlers who prey on the farms in this rugged terrain.

On the snowy slopes of the Drakensberg a woolly coat serves well in winter

A steam engine ascends the steep gradients to Barkly East

Clouds gather over Free State farmland

Land, light and water in the Orange Free State

Bread being the staff of life, wheat was one of the first grain crops that the early settlers at the Cape tried to cultivate. With the winter rains of the region, wheat flourished and the south-western Cape is still a primary wheat-producing area.

The open plains and light but fertile soils of the Orange Free State made her a potentially perfect wheat-growing area, although summer rainfall would seem to preclude success. In later years, however, the introduction of massive water conservation schemes has enabled wheat production to soar to the point where the Orange Free State now produces one third of the country's total crop.

Painted hut along the national road in the Orange Free State

Field of sun flowers near Warden, Orange Free State

Today the extensively cultivated plains of the Orange Free State yield quantities of sunflowers *(Helianthus annus)* and wheat, while deep below the surface lies a harvest of a more metallic nature – the Orange Free State goldfields which account for some 33 per cent of South Africa's gold production.

The irrigated farmlands surrounding the province's capital city, Bloemfontein, belie their recent emergence: little over 100 years ago massive herds of game, notably antelope, grazed undisturbed on these flat, rolling grasslands, characterised by an uninterrupted 360° view of the horizon.

In 1860, to commemorate the visit to South Africa of Queen Victoria's son, Prince Alfred, one Andrew Bain organised 'the greatest hunt in history' here. The bloody consequence of this outing is preserved in the Fehr Collection in the Castle in Cape Town which shows a scene from the hunt which accounted for the lives of some 4 000 antelope, all slaughtered in a single day.

The huts of the Ndebele are traditionally painted with eye-catching designs, cubist in style, in various shades of black, grey, white, brown, yellow and red. For the women, whose job it is to paint the houses, these colours were readily available in the natural ochres and pigments of their environment.

In the present-day, however, Western influence is evident not only in the painting materials which have encouraged the use of bright primary colours, but also in the modern motifs incorporated into this traditional art form. The women intersperse their familiar patterns with road signs, aeroplanes and other symbols drawn from the technological age.

Each spring the walls are either freshened or entirely new paintings are superimposed upon the old. For the most part the artists are young girls about to be married who continue in this tradition that is passed from mother to daughter.

The Ndebele sense of colour and design extends to dress as well. The women bind their legs in spectacular fashion from knee to ankle and their arms from elbow to wrist with brass rings. About their necks they wear bulky beaded hoops, and their other ornamental beadwork is now part of a growing tourist trade.

Boldly patterned Ndebele homestead

After the harvest the wheat farmers of the Orange Free State plough their fields and the land loses its golden covering of stubble. These lands are punctuated by the prominent white sandstone 'koppies' so characteristic of both the Karoo and the Free State.

These flat-topped ridges represent the legacy of a massive lava flow which covered the plains with basalt some 190 million years ago. Today the basalt lava forms a protective cap for the sandstone hills which are the only relief to an otherwise eternally flat plain.

Much of the Orange Free State is devoted to maize, wheat and small grains; also to be found here is the sunflower whose bloom is the emblem of this province and whose seed yields a valuable oil.

A farm-worker returns home

Ploughed field near Harrismith, Orange Free State
The men who simply work the land

overleaf: The 'Golden Gate', Orange Free State

Bustling Johannesburg

Egoli – the city of gold – lit by fire from heaven

Johannesburg . . . sprawling metropolis of over two million

Johannesburg, it is true, was built on gold. But in 1986 the 'Golden City' is due to celebrate its centennial and after 100 eventful years has well and truly outgrown the limits of this description.

Johannesburg together with neighbouring Soweto comprises over two million people and is today the commercial and industrial hub of South Africa.

In this big, brash city scores of cultures have met and mingled; although the style is often American and the manners frequently British, the atmosphere remains uniquely South African.

Sky-scraping to the wealth of the Rand

Kieries raised in the co-ordinated rhythm of the dance

Mine dancers at Welkom

There are 400 000 black miners on the Rand, most of whom migrate from their homes in neighbouring countries as contract workers. They, together with South Africa's own mineworkers, represent a huge cross-section of southern Africa's indigenous peoples. Maintaining their cultural identities, the various ethnic groups compete in the famed Mine Dances. Each performs one of its own traditional dances and the display culminates in a statement of the miners' urban amalgamation – the slap-stamping rhythm of the famous gum-boot dance.

Shaft of City Deep Mine – a skeleton of steel breaks the city skyline

Wind-eroded remnants of a mine dump on the outskirts of Johannesburg

Pouring molten gold into ingots, 99,5% pure

The search continues . . .

In 1978 South Africa mined 24 849 734 ounces of gold (704 479 kilograms). At the average price for the year of R168,90 per ounce this earned a total of just under R4 200 million – contributing more than 12 cents to every rand of the country's wealth.

Small wonder that Johannesburg, centre of the world's richest gold-bearing reef, is known as the 'Golden City'. To visit the labyrinthian excavations tunnelled beneath the city is literally and figuratively to make a pilgrimage to Johannesburg's foundations.

Established in 1886 following the discovery of gold by one George Harrison, the city has grown from a mining boom-town to one of the commercial capitals of the world.

The South African gold mining industry can lay claim to several world records. At Western Deep Levels mining is taking place at depths of 3 608 metres below the surface, where rock pressure is intense and constant air conditioning keeps temperatures just bearable. The highest yield of any single mine is the Crown Mines Ltd which has produced a record 1,4 million kilograms of gold. South Africa, too, has the highest mine dump – a startling 109 metres tall. She is also a leader in mine technology.

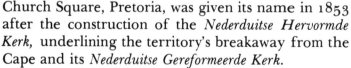
The Voortrekker Monument, outside Pretoria

Church Square, Pretoria, was given its name in 1853 after the construction of the *Nederduitse Hervormde Kerk,* underlining the territory's breakaway from the Cape and its *Nederduitse Gereformeerde Kerk.*

Here also stands a statue of Paul Kruger, the last president of the Transvaal Republic and the man generally recognised as one of the greatest figures Afrikanerdom has produced. The impact of his legacy proved to be a potent factor in the fostering of Afrikaner nationalism.

Commissioned by the South African authorities in 1910, Sir Herbert Baker, prestigious architect of Rhodes Memorial in Cape Town, proceeded with plans for what was at the time the largest building in the country. In an undertaking which would have seemed impossible 30 years before, the construction was carried out using only South African materials. Flanked by a modified Renaissance façade, the twin towers of the Union Buildings were conceived by Sir Herbert to symbolise the two major white language groups in South Africa, English and Afrikaans.

Union Buildings, Pretoria . . . seat of executive government

Once a market-place, Church Square in Pretoria

Detail from the relief carvings on the Kruger statue

The desire for freedom which in 1837 drove the Voortrekkers northwards in their wagons, culminated in the creation of the first *'Zuid-Afrikaansche Republiek'* with Pretoria as its capital. The Afrikaner was finally free of the imperial British yoke.

The independent spirit fostered by the trek itself did not diminish with the attainment of the dream. Conflict continued in a struggle between the Boers and their own authorities. Only in 1859, seven years after even the British had recognised the independence of the Republic, did the *Volksraad* (people's council) meet united in its capital.

Today the heroism of the Trekkers is commemorated in the Voortrekker Monument erected in their honour between 1938 and 1949. This huge mausoleum bears a granite cenotaph on which is inscribed *'Ons vir jou Suid-Afrika'* – words which are today incorporated in the national anthem. The plaque is so positioned that each year at noon on the 16th of December, the anniversary of the Battle of Blood River, sunlight strikes the inscription.

Pretoria takes its name from an early president, A. W. J. Pretorius. From modest beginnings the city has become a dual seat of power: it is the administrative capital of the entire Republic and also the capital of the Transvaal. Its eminence as a seat of power has attracted research laboratories, places of learning (the University of Pretoria has more students than any other in the country) and a large population.

Renowned as 'jacaranda city', its 50 000 jacarandas bathe the city in mauve late each spring. The first trees were imported from Rio de Janeiro before the turn of the century.

Oom Paul looms above a hardy Boer follower

93

A familiar sight in South Africa, the baobab

The Bushveld of the Northern Transvaal

North of Pietersburg, cattle-ranching centre of the Transvaal, lies the 'Bushveld' and it is in this region that the traveller encounters the fantastical baobab or 'Kremetartboom' (*Adansonia digitata*). In the drier parts of the African savannah, the baobab is unmistakable and its size and shape have shrouded it in legend. African folklore has it that the Creator, dissatisfied with the baobab's appearance, cast it from the Garden and it landed head first with its roots in the air.

Seeds of the large, black fruit yield cream-of-tartar, used by Africans to concoct a refreshing drink believed to have both medicinal and magical properties. In view of its stature, it is not surprising that a 'tea' from the bark is believed to impart power to a man.

A Zulu matron heavily bedecked in beads

Traditional Venda homesteads with soccer jerseys out to dry

Tzaneen tea plantation
Tsonga witchdoctor with cowrie shell headband

To the east of Pietersburg, on the lush green slopes of the Drakensberg, lies Tzaneen. Today an important tea-growing centre, Tzaneen is believed to have found its name in a Tsonga word for 'in the basket', graphically describing the town's nestling in a hollow on the south bank of the Letaba River.

Further north lie the Soutpansberg, widely inhabited by the Venda who arrived in the area possibly as late as the seventeenth century. They soon became renowned as craftsmen, skilful smiths, pot-makers and builders.

For defensive reasons they built their stone-walled villages on raised ground. Of the various tribes who waged war against the Venda, the Tsonga became their most bitter enemy. The Tsonga were powerful warriors and skilful hunters. Armed with assegais, clubs and packs of dogs, the men hunted for the pot. But at other times, specialist hunters, protected by powerful magical rites performed by their witchdoctors, stalked the great beasts of the bush and water – the elephant and the hippopotamus.

The so-called witchdoctors are better described as 'diviners' for they are believed to be able to predict and heal a great number of ills – psychological and social for the most part.

Diviners are called to their profession after signs such as epilepsy or a long history of illness are interpreted as a call by the ancestors. Their training is long and rigorous. They study under an older man or woman acknowledged as a diviner until ready to be diviners in their own right.

They wear special dress that proclaims his or her rôle. This differs from tribe to tribe but most wear distinctive headdresses (see opposite) and crossed beaded straps or thongs of goat skin across their chests.

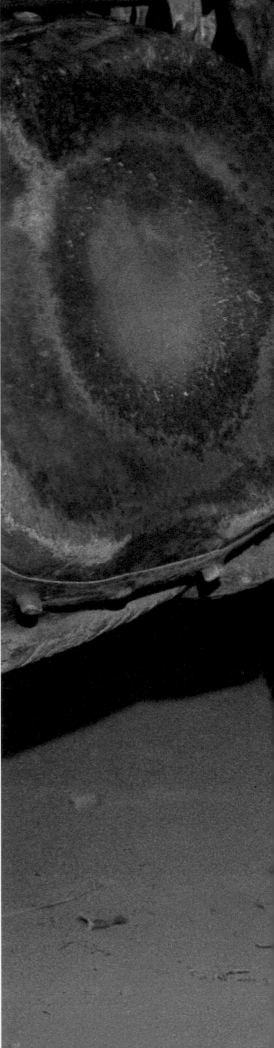

Venda maidens undergo two initiation ceremonies, the first when they reach puberty, and the second when they are of marriageable age. This latter rite, known as the *domba,* culminates in the young women forming a long line and dancing the sinuous 'python' dance to the insistent beat of a special drum (see right).

As many as 200 girls may participate in the *domba* depending on the chief's ability to cater lavishly for the event. The school generally lasts for three long months during which they undergo tuition preparing them for their rôle as adults. Through song, instruction and mimed tableaux they learn of sex and childbirth, of their duties and responsibilities as women. When not dancing or being instructed, the girls work hard in the fields and are an important source of labour.

Approaching storm in the Kruger National Park

The mosquito and the dread tsetse fly (*Glossina* spp.) were natural conservationists ensuring that man strayed into the Eastern Transvaal only at his peril. The subtropical 'Lowveld' remained out of bounds until the discovery of the port at nearby Lourenço Marques (now Maputo) and of gold in the Transvaal tempted some to blaze transport trails across this hot, low-lying region.

Men such as Paul Kruger and R. K. Loveday soon came to recognise the threat to the area. The natural wardens would require human assistance if the area was to remain unblemished. Consequently in 1898, the 'Sabie Game Reserve' was declared a protected area. The first years of this forerunner of the Kruger National Park were troubled ones, encompassing the Anglo-Boer War, so that it was not until 1902 that Colonel James Stevenson-Hamilton was appointed as the first warden.

Yellow-throated Longclaw (*Macronyx croceus*)

Witgatboom (Boscia albitrunca)

The bewildered reaction of indigenous hunters and herders was picturesquely captured in the praise-name they conferred upon the diminutive Dubliner, short of temper and stature. 'Skukuza', they called him, which means 'he who has turned everything upside-down'. The name is preserved today in that of one of the many tourist camps which can be found in the Kruger National Park, first opened to the public in 1927.

Where animals come to drink

101

Challenging stare of the Martial Eagle

The imperious Martial Eagle, seemingly trousered in spotted ermine, ranks among the largest eagles in the world. The female, larger than her mate, weighs in at about 6,5 kilograms.

The smaller Crowned Eagle, with its powerful legs and talons, can catch and carry prey up to four times its own mass, but the Martial Eagle is equipped only to prey upon fast-moving birds and small mammals – notice the hare in the photograph. And, with its superb eyesight, it is a supremely efficient hunter.

Its distinctive voice, a 'kloo-ee, kloo-ee, kloo-ee, kloo-ee, ku-lee' followed by a throaty 'quolp' is heard over most of Africa south of the Sahara.

Fondly known as 'LBR', the Lilac-breasted Roller

Sprawling over an area of nearly 20 000 kilometres from the southern borders of the Transvaal to the Limpopo in the north, the Kruger National Park offers a wider variety of wildlife than any other game reserve in the world.

The park is equipped to handle a vast influx of tourists; its many lodges and extensive network of well-serviced roads make for luxurious as well as exciting viewing. If one wishes to commune with the wilds at first hand there are foot-tours which bring one into close proximity with all the beasts – from the elusive dik-dik to the majestic lion.

The wild dog, although smaller than the lion and leopard, must take its place beside them as a deadly and effective hunter. Rarely seen alone or in pairs, they move in packs of up to 90 individuals which prowl the African savannah and hunt together.

Replete, a leopard takes its ease

Wild dogs on the alert

Once a threatened species, the African buffalo now browses in safety in the Kruger National Park

The management of the game protected in the Kruger National Park is entrusted to a highly qualified team of wardens and conservationists who must take important decisions concerning the welfare of their charges. One of the most explosive and controversial issues is whether or not to cull the Park's mightiest inhabitant, the elephant, in the interests of its own survival and that of the environment.

An aggressive young leopard

The elegant giraffe stoops to drink

Bull elephant pictured near the Letaba camp

In the Eastern Transvaal, South Africa's 'Highveld' plateau tumbles for 1 000 metres down fecund, green gorges, pot-holed canyons, and majestic waterfalls, to the rich and fertile subtropical 'Lowveld'. This is the Drakensberg range's eastern escarpment, the 'edge of the world', and here breathtaking scenery and relics of an eventful past combine to produce an aura of magic. Perhaps, on a walk at the foot of such colourfully-named mountainsides as Long Tom Pass, Magoebaskloof and Swartbooi's Path, a modern-day prospector will trip over a stone as valuable as the six kilogram gold nugget found at Pilgrim's Rest a century ago.

The Berlin Falls drop a vertiginous 80 metres

Lonely farmhouse near Carolina in the Eastern Transvaal

View from the Long Tom Pass

Misty green forests of the Eastern Transvaal

The Blyde River plunges until it emerges from the mountains. Fed by the high rainfall of the highlands, it has the highest run-off of any perennial stream in the land.

Behind the naming of the Blyde and Treur Rivers lies a touching story. History has it that in 1844 Andries Hendrik Potgieter left his wagon train and set off across the mountains in search of the Portuguese at Delagoa Bay. Many weeks passed but there was no sign of the Boer leader. Despondent, those he had left behind broke camp and named the river beside which their laager had been, the 'Treurrivier' – River of Sorrow. Not long after, they were overtaken by Potgieter and his men, and aptly named the river by which they now camped the 'Blyderivier' – River of Joy.

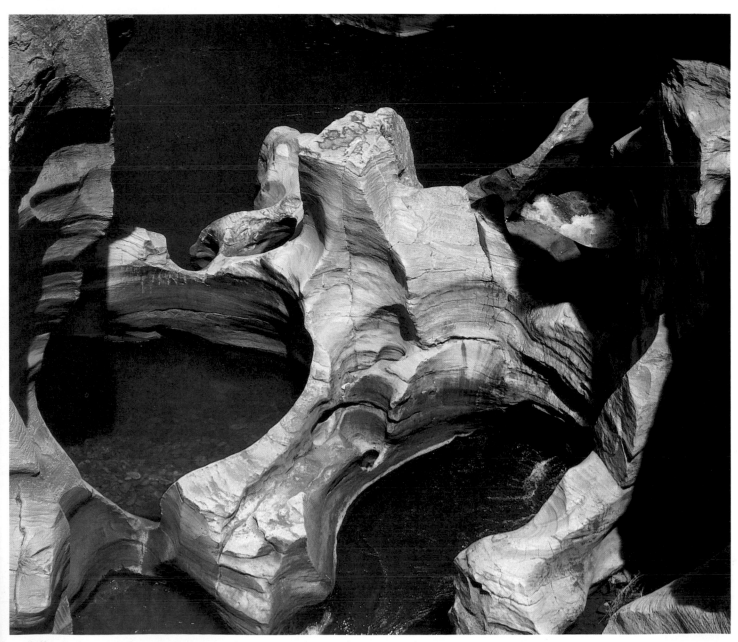

A falls (left) and Bourke's Luck Potholes (above) on the Blyde River

Above the confluence of the Blyde and Treur Rivers is Bourke's Luck Potholes where pebbles and boulders tumbled by the swift-flowing stream have scoured and sculpted the bizarre-shaped rocks.

Early prospectors found nuggets lying among the stones in the potholes although now the nearby gold mine, Bourke's Luck, stands silent.

Just beyond the swirling waters of Bourke's Luck Potholes the Blyde River breaks through into a spectacular gorge and then enters one of the most beautiful canyons in Africa. The Blyde River Canyon – dazzling in its greenness, dominated by the imposing formations of the Three Rondavels and awesome silence.

But the Blyde River is only one of many rivers in this area that find their way to the Lowveld: others include the Waterval, which plunges in vertical twin falls 56 metres over a precipice, and the Debegeni which cascades down slopes. Indeed everywhere there are crystal-clear creeks, winding through towering indigenous forests interrupted only where man has levelled and planted tea plantations and citrus groves.

The Lowveld itself lies east of the great escarpment in the northern Transvaal and stretches northwards to the Limpopo and Rhodesia-Zimbabwe beyond. In summer malaria is prevalent and coupled with the hot subtropical climate did not make this region attractive for settlement. Many farmers spent the summers in the Highveld and took their cattle to feed on the long grasses of the Lowveld when the air grew cooler and mosquitoes were no longer abundant.

The Three Rondavels in the Blyde River Canyon

The Blyde River from World's End

Source of mining town news

Antiquated link with the outside world

Main Street, Pilgrim's Rest

Throughout the 1860s there were rumours of gold in the Transvaal and Karl Mauch had actually found alluvial gold in the Blyde River Valley in 1867; but it was only in 1874 that a real strike was made – at a site that came to be called Pilgrim's Rest. A mad rush ensued, prospectors braving the trip across the Lowveld, undaunted by the threat of sleeping sickness, malaria and all the terrors of the unknown in pursuit of El Dorado. They were not to be disappointed: over a period of four years (1874-1878) 1 500 of these men panned £1 500 000 worth of alluvial gold from Pilgrim's Creek, a tributary of the Blyde River.

A vibrant mining town mushroomed in the magnificent surrounds; and although the mine was closed in 1971, the town is maintained as a charming relic of the first of the great South African gold rushes.

Today timber is the new wealth in these parts and thousands of hectares round Pilgrim's Rest, Sabie, Henriksdal and Graskop have been planted with pines and eucalyptus.

As is the case with most traditional societies in Africa, Swazi society is based on a patrilineal kinship system (kinship is traced through the male). What distinguishes this tribe from others, however, is that the centre of power lies traditionally not only in the Chief but also in the Queen Mother.

Together they stand as symbolic parents of the people. The chief, known as *Ingwenyama,* 'the lion', and his mother, called *Indlovukati,* the 'lady elephant', share responsibility for the dispensation of justice and the control of the military and each plays an essential rôle in the vital rain-making ceremony.

In fact, the rôle of mothers in general in Swazi society is such that there is a popular riddle: 'If your mother and your wife are drowning, which one should you save? Answer: Your mother – you can always get another wife.'

The Swazi share close ties of blood, language and culture with the Zulu, but the main dividing factor is that the Swazi unlike the Zulu were never conquerors. That is not to say that the Swazi were not fighting men. They imitated Shaka's reorganisation of his army along lines of age group allegiances and direct control by the chief. Led by the great Chief Mswati the Swazi raided as far afield as what is now Rhodesia-Zimbabwe. But they did not appear to share the Zulu ambition of forging a mighty empire. The main purpose of their raids was to win spoils, for the most part cattle, and for the sheer excitement of battle.

Swazi kraal in the Eastern Transvaal

Zulu potter at Babanango

The ochred coiffure of a Zulu woman

The Zulu are the most widely known of Africa's traditional societies. Armed with short, stabbing assegais and bare-footed in battle, the Zulu warriors rose to prominence guided by the supreme military genius of the legendary Shaka.

Ascending to the throne in 1816, Shaka, with the backing of the war machine built up by Dingiswayo before him, evolved a military strategy such as had never before been used in this part of Africa. An army that was based upon regimentation into age groups rather than on local and district allegiances, swept through south-eastern Africa, its prowess a myth in its own time.

Under the hegemony of Shaka, his warriors created a chaos of mass-slaughter and forced migrations. Such famous chiefdoms as that of the Matabele, Basotho and Ngoni evolved as a result of the *Difaqane* (forced migrations). In spite of the glory that Shaka brought to the Zulu nation, his tyranny led to his murder at the hand of his brother, Dingaan, in 1820.

Traditional arrangement of a Zulu kraal in the Drakensberg

Zulu impis in authentic battledress

In full regalia, a Sotho dancer performs

Dance, poetry, music and song are an integral part of ritual festivals in southern Africa. They are also an essential element in the celebration of events connected with every aspect of life. Besides the massed dances which are perhaps better known, there are masquerades set to the music of drums and rattles or song. In these, stereotyped characters in familiar costume enact stories from tribal folklore.

African dance not only expresses emotion, it gives a deep sense of pleasure to the dancers and to those watching.

In southern Africa traditional dance is principally performed as a means of recreation. It is not generally representational nor need it have any ritual import. People may dance at a funeral, a wedding, a birth.

Traditional dance is characterised by its discipline: rhythmic chanting and stamping in strict unison usually performed by a large group. If men dance, the women form a clapping and singing chorus; if the women dance, the men, in turn, provide accompaniment. Under the light of a full moon, people gather readily to enjoy the communal pleasure of dancing with drinking and courtship as side attractions.

When the earth trembles with the chanting and the foot-pounding of several hundred men, the Zulus aptly liken it to the crashing of the waves on the seashore.

An unmarried Zulu maiden dancing at the *Shembe* festival

The black herders of Africa value their cattle above all else – as a symbol of status, the principal measure of wealth and as a means of exchange. In the practice of *lobola,* bride-wealth, the prospective son-in-law gives his bride's family cattle. But this is not payment for a 'bought' wife, it is a reciprocal arrangement; the cattle received in *lobola* will be used by the bride's brother when he, in turn, wishes to take a wife.

Traditional homestead

With briefcase and walking-stick – the cattle executive

122

Isolated country church

The tasks of yesterday, the fashions of today

There are three game reserves in Natal whose charming names vie with their natural beauty and the wildlife. The biggest is the Mkuze Game Reserve which derives its name from the aromatic trees which line the banks of the river flowing through the sanctuary. Then there is the Umfolozi Game Reserve, named for the two rivers which 'zig-zag' through it. Finally, the 'Hluhluwe', melodious name of the *Liana dalbergia armata* – more popularly known as the 'monkey rope'.

Social drinking   Favourite pastime – wallowing

124

Indigenous 'cattle' of Africa – the eland

White rhino in the Umfolozi Game Reserve

Umfolozi Game Reserve is credited with nursing the endangered white (or square-lipped) rhino back to healthy numbers. This more docile cousin of the black rhino was on the verge of extinction when the Umfolozi was proclaimed a reserve in 1897. Today a population of one thousand is maintained in the park, and the surplus is shipped to other game reserves around the world. So far 500 white rhinos have been 'exported' in this fashion.

An egret hunched in the breeze

The giraffe finds its food far above the heads of most other animals

A flurry of feathers in self defence

Distinctive hindquarters of the impala

Most fearsome of the riverine predators, the crocodile is present in most of the wild waters of Africa, but only the Nile crocodile is indigenous to South Africa.

Through the millennia, this relic from prehistoric times has developed several unique adaptative features to suit its semi-aquatic lifestyle. Legs held close to the body, it is the powerful tail that is used to propel the reptile through the water. A further adaptation is the cunning positioning of eyes, nostrils and ear openings on the flattened upper surface of the head so that the crocodile can see, hear and breathe as it floats, log-like, all but submerged below the water's surface. Children in Africa grow up with the fear of those two yellow 'leaves' that always float side by side past the river banks.

Leviathan of ancient and modern myth, the crocodile was revered by the Ancient Egyptians and mummified remains of the reptiles have been found in tombs uncovered during archaeological excavations.

Primeval menace of the crocodile

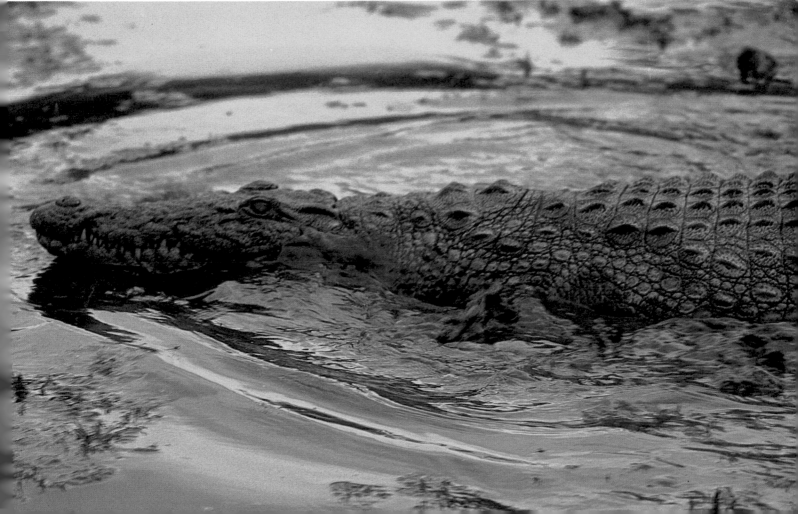

The Drakensberg 'Dragon-mountain' is in reality the crumbling face of the escarpment which falls away from South Africa's inland plateau. In the north it divides the Transvaal Highveld from the subtropical Lowveld, and in Natal, where the massive cliff faces are at their most prominent, the range separates Natal from Lesotho. Here the *ulundi* 'heights' reach to the roof of South Africa, and the frequently snow-capped Thabantshonyana rises to a height of 3 482 metres.

The mountain chain consists of basaltic lava, spewed over the older and brightly-coloured sandstone perhaps 200 million years ago. The high lands of the Drakensberg are the source of many perennial rivers, the range itself providing a watershed between the west-flowing and east-flowing rivers of South Africa.

When the lower strata of sediments of today's Drakensberg were swamps, great reptilian creatures trod the mud. In time the region became more arid and these animals died out. However, their footprints, bones, partial skeletons and skulls prove indisputably that these huge beasts roamed here.

Within the refuge of the Drakensberg Bushman painters continued their craft until relatively recently. The average age of the paintings discovered in the Natal Drakensberg escarpment is a modest 200 years.

The Drakensberg offered abundant shelter and food and here the community survived long enough to record the violence and warfare which becomes a prominent feature of southern African history – the arrival first of the black man and then of the white.

The Devil's Tooth in late afternoon, Drakensberg
The Tugela waterfall crashing down the Amphitheatre

overleaf: Storm over the Amphitheatre, Drakensberg